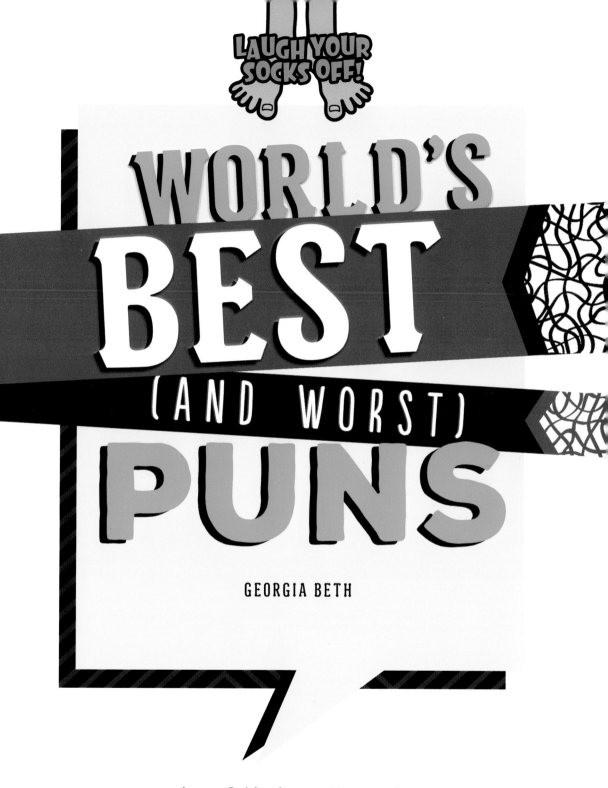

LAUGH YOUR SOCKS OFF!

WORLD'S BEST (AND WORST) PUNS

GEORGIA BETH

Lerner Publications ◆ Minneapolis

Q What did the duck say after watching his favorite TV show?

A It **QUACKS** me up!

Lerner Publications Company
A division of Lerner Publishing Group, Inc.
241 First Avenue North
Minneapolis, MN 55401 USA

For reading levels and more information, look up this title at www.lernerbooks.com.

Main body text set in Billy Infant Regular.
Typeface provided by SparkyType.

Library of Congress Cataloging-in-Publication Data

Names: Beth, Georgia, author.
Title: World's best (and worst) puns / Georgia Beth.
Description: Minneapolis : Lerner Publications, [2018] | Series: Laugh your socks off!
Identifiers: LCCN 2017014149 (print) | LCCN 2017031507 (ebook) | ISBN 9781512483550 (eb pdf) |
    ISBN 9781512483505 (lb : alk. paper)
Subjects: LCSH: Puns and punning—Juvenile literature. | Plays on words—Juvenile literature.
Classification: LCC PN6231.P8 (ebook) | LCC PN6231.P8 B48 2018 (print) | DDC 818/.602—dc23

LC record available at https://lccn.loc.gov/2017014149

Manufactured in the United States of America
1-43348-33168-8/16/2017

Q What's smarter than a talking bird?

A A spelling bee.

Q Why is a fish easy to weigh?

A Because it has its own **SCALES**.

Q Why is it hard to shock a cow?

A They've **HERD** it all.

Q What kind of music do frogs play at parties?

A Hip-hop.

 Q When is a baby good at basketball?

 A When it's **DRIBBLING**

 Q Why don't more people become ballerinas?

 A Because it's **TUTU** hard.

 Q Did you hear about the angry gymnast?

A He totally **FLIPPED**.

Q What is a sheep's favorite sport?

A Baaadminton.

Q What did the glove say to the baseball?

A Catch you later!

Q How do surfers say hello?

A They **WAVE**.

Q Why is tennis so loud?

A Players really raise a **RACKET**.

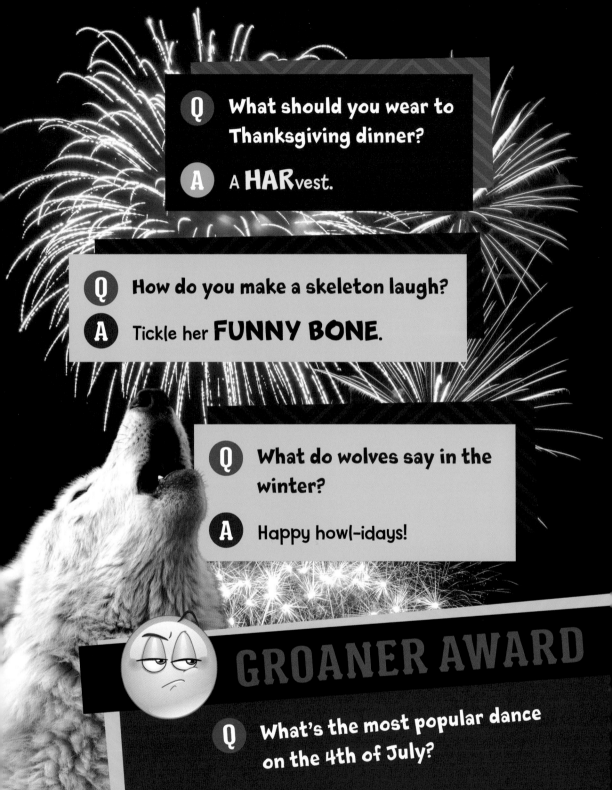

Q What should you wear to Thanksgiving dinner?

A A **HAR**vest.

Q How do you make a skeleton laugh?

A Tickle her **FUNNY BONE**.

Q What do wolves say in the winter?

A Happy howl-idays!

GROANER AWARD

Q What's the most popular dance on the 4th of July?

A Indepen-dance!

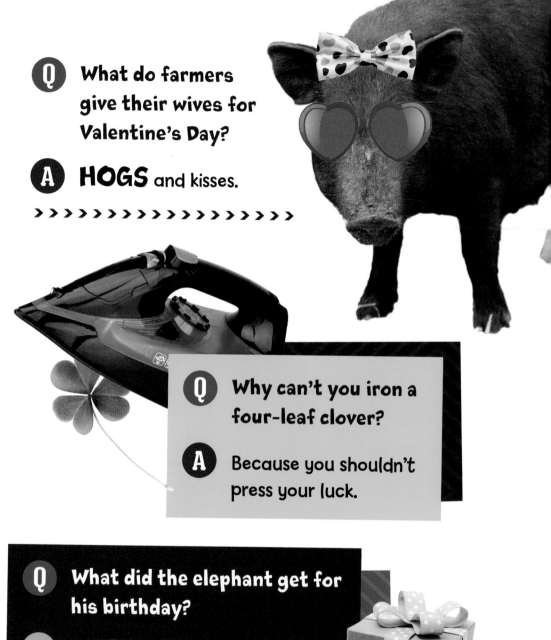

Q What do farmers give their wives for Valentine's Day?

A **HOGS** and kisses.

>>>>>>>>>>>>>>>>>>>

Q Why can't you iron a four-leaf clover?

A Because you shouldn't press your luck.

Q What did the elephant get for his birthday?

A A **TRUNKFUL** of presents.

Q What did the lightning bolt say to the other lightning bolt?

A You're **SHOCKING**!

 Q Why did the germs cross the microscope?

 A To get to the other **SLIDE**.

KNEE-SLAPPER

Q How do scientists freshen their breath?

A With **EXPERI-MINTS**!

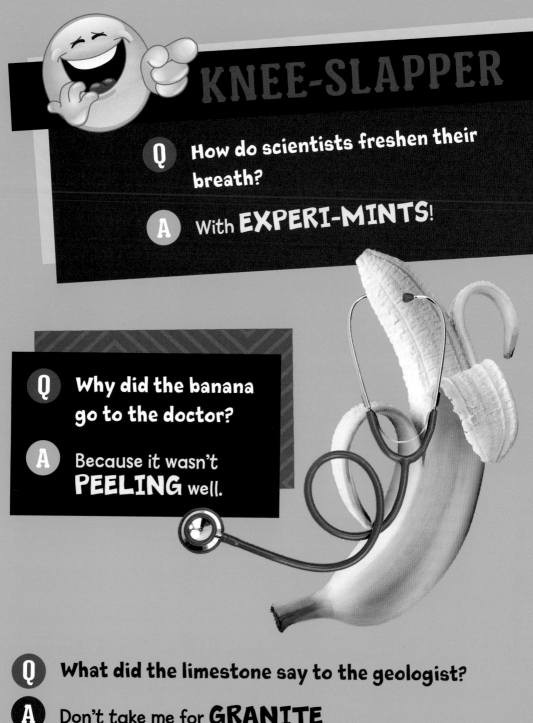

Q Why did the banana go to the doctor?

A Because it wasn't **PEELING** well.

Q What did the limestone say to the geologist?

A Don't take me for **GRANITE**.

Q What did one math book say to the other after it complained?

A Don't bother me. **I'VE GOT MY OWN PROBLEMS.**

Q Why did the girl wear glasses during math class?

A Because it improves **DIVISION.**

Q What can you do if you don't understand your math homework?

A Ask your teacher to **SUM IT UP** for you.

Q What subject in school is easy for a witch?

A Spelling.

 Q Why did the teacher wear sunglasses?

A Because her students were so **BRIGHT**.

›››››››››››››››››››››››

 Q What kind of school do giants go to?

A High school.

‹‹‹‹‹‹‹‹‹‹‹‹‹‹‹‹‹‹‹‹‹‹‹‹

 Q How do you get straight As?

A Use a **RULER**.

 Q Why do magicians get good grades?

 A They know how to answer **TRICK QUESTIONS**.

Q Which dinosaurs were the best police officers?

A Tricera-**COPS**.

Q What kind of dinosaur can you ride in a rodeo?

A A **BRONCO**-saurus.

Q What was the scariest dinosaur?

A The **TERROR**-dactyl.

Q Why did the velociraptor let the brontosaurus win?

A Because no one likes a **SAUR** loser.

>>>>>>>>>>>>>>>>>>>>>>>>>>>>>>>>>>>

Q What do you call a dinosaur with no eyes?

A Do-ya-think-he-saw-us.

GROANER AWARD

Q What do you get when you cross a dinosaur with fireworks?

A **DINO**-mite.

KNEE-SLAPPER

Q Why don't aliens eat clowns?

A Because they taste funny.

Q What kind of plates do they use in space?

A Flying saucers.

Q When is the moon the heaviest?

A When it's **FULL**.

Q How do you organize a space party?

A You **PLANET**.

Q What do astronauts like to read?

A **COMET** books.

Q What do you call fruit in space?

A Coco-nauts.

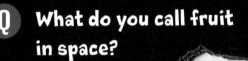

Q What type of music are balloons scared of?

A Pop music.

Q What do you get when you put a radio in the freezer?

A Cool music.

Q Why are pirates great singers?

A They can hit the **HIGH C**s.

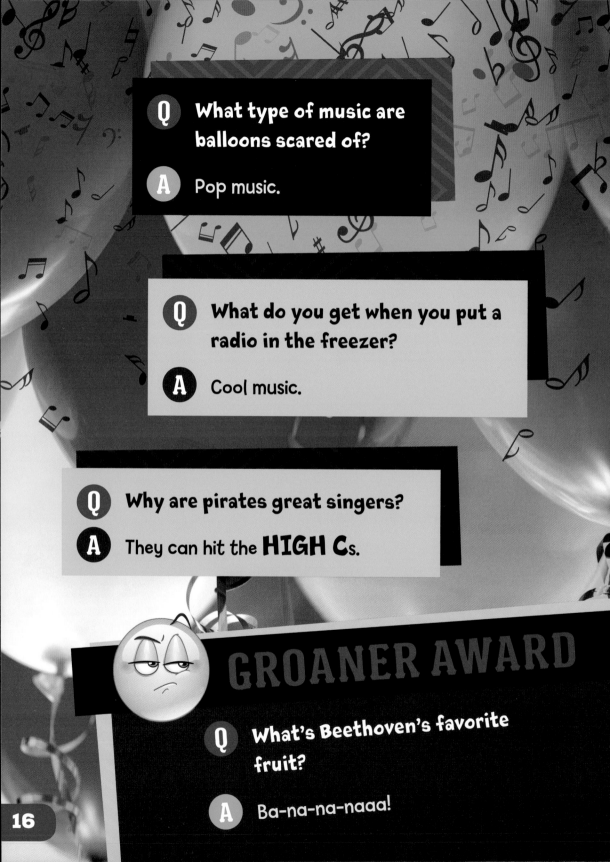

GROANER AWARD

Q What's Beethoven's favorite fruit?

A Ba-na-na-naaa!

Q What's the most musical part of a turkey?

A The **DRUMSTICK**.

Q Why did the musician put his head inside the piano?

A He wanted to **PLAY IT BY EAR**.

Q What do you call a cow that plays a musical instrument?

A A **MOO**-sician.

Q Why couldn't the librarian go to the movies?

A His weekend was **ALL BOOKED**.

Q What do you get when you throw a million books into the ocean?

A A **TITLE** wave.

Q Did you read the book about Mount Everest?

A It was a real **CLIFF-HANGER**.

KNEE-SLAPPER

Q Is it time to hit the books?

A No. Violence is never the answer!

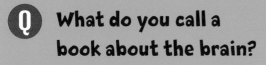

Q What do you call a
book about the brain?

A A mind reader.

<<<<<<<<<<<<<<<<<<<<<<<

Q Who should you get
mad at when a book
falls on your head?

A You can only blame
YOUR SHELF.

Q Why are librarians always
buying new books about birds?

A Because they keep **FLYING
OFF THE SHELF.**

Q What do librarians take with
them when they go fishing?

A Bookworms.

Q How do artists greet one another?

A They say, **"YELLOW!"**

Q What do you call a painting by a cat?

A A paw-trait.

Q What did the critics say about the monster's painting?

A It's a master-beast.

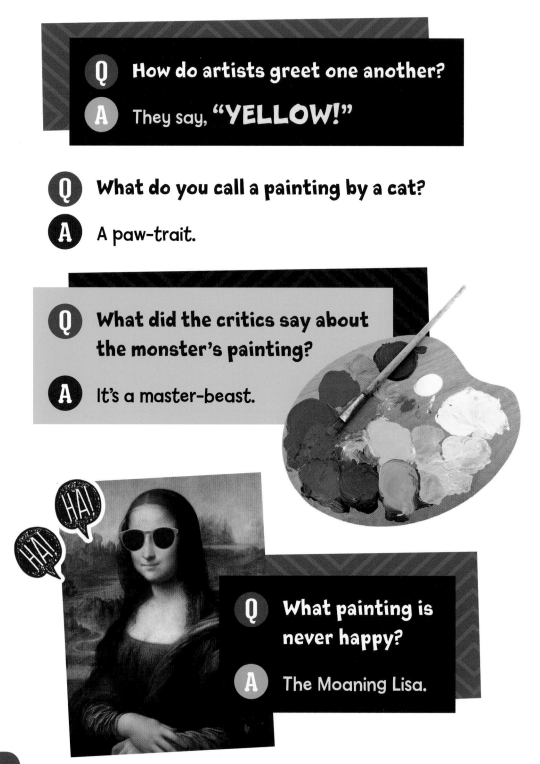

Q What painting is never happy?

A The Moaning Lisa.

Q Which animals are famous painters?

A Pablo **PIG**-casso and Vincent van **GOAT**.

Q What did the bacon say to the tomato?

A **LETTUCE** get together.

Q What did the baby corn say to the mama corn?

A Where's **POP?**

<<<<<<<<<<<<<<<<<<<<

Q What did the mama tomato say to the baby tomato?

A Catch up!

Q Why was the cucumber mad?

A Because it was in a **PICKLE.**

Q What do you call cheese that's not yours?

A **NACHO** cheese.

Q What is a frog's favorite cold drink?

A **CROAK**-a-cola.

Q Why don't eggs tell jokes?

A They'd **CRACK EACH OTHER UP.**

24